Original title:
Life: As Explained by a Sloth

Copyright © 2025 Creative Arts Management OÜ
All rights reserved.

Author: Nolan Kingsley
ISBN HARDBACK: 978-1-80566-067-5
ISBN PAPERBACK: 978-1-80566-362-1

Fluttering Hearts in a Calm Canopy

In the treetops, hanging still,
Time drips slowly like a thrill,
With leafy greens and sunny beams,
I take my time, I chase my dreams.

Leaves whisper secrets, oh so sweet,
I munch and lounge, it can't be beat,
A gentle breeze, a quiet sigh,
While critters rush, I simply lie.

The world zooms past at breakneck speed,
But I'll just stretch, that's all I need,
Finding joy in every glance,
With every nap, I take my chance.

Hurry not, in this bright space,
Why race ahead when slow's the pace?
With every blink, there's joy to borrow,
In a calm world, why not just follow?

The Philosophy of Hanging Around

In branches high, we sway and grin,
The world below, a dizzy spin.
We ponder deep while hanging free,
The art of chill, our guarantee.

Why rush ahead, miss joys that bloom?
We stretch and yawn, feel sunlight's room.
With lazy laughs, we take our chance,
In slow-motion, life's a dance.

Serenity Under the Canopy

Beneath the leaves, a quiet space,
No need to hurry, no wicked race.
We snooze and dream, all wrapped in peace,
In slothful stillness, worries cease.

The whispers of the winds do tease,
While sunbeams play through rustling trees.
A casual glance at the daytime show,
A hammock life where slow can flow.

Time's Gentle Embrace

With every hour, we take our time,
From twig to branch, we gently climb.
The clock ticks softly, a lazy beat,
With every moment, life tastes sweet.

We see the world move fast and bold,
But wisdom whispers, the best is slow.
In moments stretched, we find our bliss,
A tasty snack becomes a kiss.

Stillness in Motion

Though we may seem to nap and gaze,
Our hearts are racing in their laze.
Each branch we grasp, a secret shared,
In stillness found, we haven't cared.

So let them hurry, let them fret,
We'll savor sun, without regret.
With every pause, we find delight,
In cozy dreams, we own the night.

Inertia in a World of Chaos

In a world that spins and whirls,
I hang out, sipping on my pearls.
The rush, the fuss, all seem so bizarre,
While I just chill beneath the stars.

People zoom past, in a crazy race,
I'm in my tree, finding my space.
What's the hurry? What's the craze?
I'll enjoy my slow, lazy days.

The Art of Taking It Slow

A leaf, a branch, my graceful throne,
I savor moments all on my own.
Others fly by, like they won't survive,
But here I am, just glad to thrive.

When the sun sets, I take a nap,
Miss the noise, but love the gap.
With minimal effort, I'm living free,
Oh, the art of slow is pure glee!

Dreams of a Languid Heart

In a dream of green, I slowly sway,
No rush to greet the dawning day.
With a yawn, I stretch, then close my eyes,
Chasing clouds, drifting in the skies.

Each small thought is a gentle breeze,
Whispering secrets through the trees.
With dreams so slow, they softly start,
I cradle the world with a languid heart.

Unrushed Rhythms of Existence

Tick-tock, oh how time can crawl,
While others dash, I take my fall.
Each second blooms, a fragrant flower,
In the stillness, I find my power.

Waves of calm in a noisy sea,
The symphony sings just for me.
As I lounge and watch the show,
I'll be the hero of the slow.

Dreaming Without Rush

In a tree so high, I take my seat,
The world below moves quick, neat.
I yawn, I stretch, oh what a view,
Why rush when dreaming will do?

Sunshine filters, a gentle tease,
Slowly swaying in the breeze.
A nap or two, what's the fuss?
In my slothful world, there's no rush.

Harmony in Leisure's Embrace

With mossy smiles, I curl up tight,
Embracing slow in morning light.
The branches sway, a lullaby,
A blissful tune as hours slip by.

I watch the ants with curious eyes,
They rush, they chase, oh what a prize!
But here I linger, calm and free,
In this rhythm, just me and me.

A Tangle of Thoughts Among Leaves

Floating gently, thoughts unwind,
Like leaves that dance, not one aligned.
What's the plan? I can't quite say,
I'm lost in slow, and that's okay.

An acorn drops, a busy bee,
Yet here I am, delightfully free.
Twisted tales within my head,
Each one woven in dreams I've fed.

The Sluggish Symphony of Surrender

A symphony of yawns and sighs,
As turtles trot and time just flies.
In nocturnal dreams, I float and sway,
Surrendered slow to the day's ballet.

The world blurs past, it's a funny scene,
While I sip time like a fragrant bean.
Each moment savored, plucked with care,
In my lazy concert, there's magic in air.

Journeys at a Snail's Pace

In the treetops where I dwell,
Adventure calls, oh can't you tell?
But with a yawn, I'll take my time,
Each leaf is perfect, every climb.

With every stretch, I ponder slow,
Why rush when there's so much to grow?
The world spins fast, but here I'll sway,
A leisurely stroll is my own way.

Navigating Life's Tranquil Currents

I float along the branches high,
Where breezes play and moments sigh.
The river of my thoughts runs deep,
In gentle curls, I find my sleep.

Waves of food just drift my way,
I snack and nap, then nap a day.
Why be in haste when sweet and slow
Is how I like my flow to go?

A Sloth's Soliloquy on Existence

What is this rush, this frantic race?
I ponder slow in my green space.
With every snack, I find a thought,
In chilled-out dreams, I'm never caught.

The clock ticks loud, can't hear the chime,
No need for speed; I'm just sublime.
With leaves for lunch and sun for cheer,
The answers come, but only near.

Unrushed Bonds in the Boughs

In branches thick, we hold our chats,
With friendships tied in leafy hats.
We take our time, no need for haste,
In laughter's hug, we find our place.

The world beneath may blare and bark,
But in our limbs, it's warm and dark.
Slow hugs and smiles linger too,
In friendly sloth-style, we'll see it through.

Cuddled Close to Contentment

In the tree, I take my time,
Each slow move feels just sublime.
A leaf or two, my tasty treat,
While friends watch on, it's quite the feat.

No hurry here, I softly sway,
The world zooms by, but I will stay.
A yawn escapes, I greet the sun,
In my own world, I have my fun.

Restful Revelations in the Canopy

As branches bend, I ponder deep,
With every nap, new dreams I keep.
A squirrel zips past, what a delight!
I chuckle softly, what a sight!

Cars rush below, they seem so mad,
I simply grin, I'm far from sad.
To live so slow, it's quite the game,
They rush for gold, I seek no fame.

The Gentle Philosophy of Pause

Why rush to move when it's so grand,
To stretch my limbs, to slowly stand?
A quirky thought, I must confess,
The art of chill, I've come to bless.

To dangle low and gaze around,
Is wisdom pure as bark is brown.
For every snack and moment shared,
The silliest things are always dared.

Hanging Around with Curiosity

What's that down there? A rustling leaf,
A playful breeze, oh what a thief!
I dangle close, my heart a race,
Exploring all this wondrous space.

From branch to branch, I slowly glide,
With every twist, I take in stride.
Curiosity, my constant friend,
Around each curve, new tales to send.

The Philosophical Pause

In a tree where time stands still,
A sloth considers all with a grin.
Should I munch on leaves or just chill?
Decisions take a minute, or maybe ten.

With a furrowed brow, he ponders slow,
The meaning of naps and the joy of the breeze.
Why rush to the ground when there's much to show?
He stretches each second with languid ease.

Whispered Tales from Above

From the branches, stories drift,
Of lazy days and sunlit dreams.
Whispers of joy, a gentle gift,
In silence, a million giggles gleam.

With a sigh, he sways in delight,
Each leaf tells a tale, a soft, sweet spin.
Pausing for thoughts that feel just right,
In this slow dance, he always wins.

Contemplations of a Cuddly Dreamer

Cuddled up in the arms of time,
A world of wonder unfolds with a yawn.
Thoughts drift like clouds, so soft and sublime,
In dreams of fruit, he's jovially drawn.

Without a care, he settles at ease,
Pondering life's great, meandering path.
A cozy heart, a spirit that frees,
Sloths live with smiles, escaping the math.

The Echoing Beat of a Slow Heart

With every tick of the lazy sun,
A heart beats soft in a steady pace.
Why hurry at all? Just have some fun!
Laughter echoes in this serene space.

Slow steps create a rhythm divine,
Every munch a symphony of glee.
In the hush of woods, life is just fine,
A joyous dance, just him and the tree.

The Lullaby of the Undisturbed

Hanging high, a cozy nook,
A sleepy sloth, with time to look.
The world spins fast, I stretch and yawn,
In my slow life, the day is drawn.

Leaves sway gently, soft and green,
Every moment, a lazy dream.
While others rush, I take my pause,
And cheer my heart with nature's cause.

Whispering Leaves

In the trees, where breezes play,
I'll lounge about the whole long day.
Branches dance with the softest hum,
But I just smile, for a nap will come.

Lazily watching clouds drift by,
Chasing the shadows in the sky.
While time ticks on in a hurried race,
I savor snacks at my favorite pace.

Silent Dreams

In the stillness, dreams unfold,
Where worries fade and hearts grow bold.
I nap so deep in a leafy bed,
With visions bright that paint my head.

Others fret about what's in store,
But I just snore and dream some more.
Adventure waits on a frozen clock,
As I slowly weave through this leafy block.

The Power of Pausing

Stop and smell the fragrant air,
With lazy grace, I lounge with flair.
While hurried folks dash all around,
I find my joy in being ground-bound.

Time's a friend when you're not in haste,
Life's sweet moments, never waste.
In my slow realm, joy multiplies,
Underneath the lazy skies.

Slow Shadows on a Sunlit Path

Sunbeams twinkle on emerald leaves,
As I meander, all time deceives.
With fuzzy limbs and a heart so bold,
I embrace the heat, not feeling cold.

Beneath the trees, shadows dance,
In this slow game, I take my chance.
Each step deliberate, each breath divine,
In this fun journey, I just recline.

Waiting for Epiphanies in the Shade

In the branches, I lounge with ease,
Ideas drift by like a gentle breeze.
Patience is golden, or so they say,
I'll think about that—maybe tomorrow, yay!

With every slow blink, I ponder and tease,
What should I do with my abundant freeze?
The world rushes by, but here I remain,
Catching sunbeams and avoiding the rain.

The Softness of Slumbering Goals

Goals are like dreams in a cozy cocoon,
Wrapped up so snug, I can snooze till noon.
They whisper sweet nothings, coax me to stay,
But waking up quick is just not my way.

As I drift between worlds, ambitions may fade,
Turning to nap-time instead of a trade.
The more that I snooze, the less I pursue,
But isn't this dreamland a goal, too?

Winding Paths of Peaceful Intent

I wander with glee on my winding trails,
Every turn a new snack, where relaxation prevails.
If haste is a race, I'm not in the game,
My compass says 'slow,' I'll keep it the same.

With purpose so mellow, I stroll at a crawl,
Embracing the journey, I'll savor it all.
Each leaf is a treasure, each branch a delight,
In my unhurried path, everything feels right.

The Unhurried Heart's Cadence

My heart beats a rhythm like a soft, slow drum,
Waltzing through hours, I find joy in the hum.
Each pulse is a giggle, each sigh a soft breeze,
The music of slowness, it always appease.

Tick-tock has a way, but I only pretend,
Time's a good friend when you've all got to spend.
In this dance of delays, I find my sweet charm,
With patience as armor, I'm safe from alarm.

Gentle Reflections from the Treetops

In the canopy, I ponder slow,
The world below, a vibrant show.
With every munch of tender leaves,
I chuckle at the rush that weaves.

A lazy stretch, a yawn so wide,
Why sprint when there's a slow glide?
The breeze tickles, I sway with ease,
Each little moment aims to please.

Chasing shadows, sunbeams play,
While friends below just rush away.
I take a nap on a sturdy limb,
Dreaming dreams of whimsy and whim.

In tranquil heights, I find my peace,
From wild chaos, I seek release.
Life's a journey, slow as a song,
In the treetops, I know I belong.

Surrendering to Stillness

In the stillness, I take my stand,
My very own slow-motion land.
Leaves flutter past as I blink twice,
Time moves slow—oh, isn't it nice?

The birds flit fast and giggle near,
But I just grin, without a fear.
I want to feel each passing hour,
Like droplets falling from a shower.

Beneath the sun, I languidly sway,
With no rush to guide my day.
Every sound a comforting tune,
In this lazy afternoon.

In a world that runs on haste,
I savor each slow, tasty taste.
A lesson in the joy of rest,
In quiet moments, I am blessed.

Beholding the Beauty of the Mundane

A flower blooms, a leaf lets go,
But look! Oh, such a splendid show!
In every twist of winding vine,
I find a spark, a sign divine.

The world whirls fast, the colors flash,
Yet I embrace the gentle clash.
An ant might scurry, but I just smile,
Let time unfold; I'll stay awhile.

With every twig and every stone,
I see how beauty's overgrown.
The simple things, they sing to me,
In every trunk, a mystery.

Pausing to catch the sunset's glow,
I relish moments, nice and slow.
In these treasures, great and small,
I find the joy that fills it all.

The Wisdom of Waiting

I sit upon my leafy throne,
With wisdom only sloths have grown.
Why rush to finish, run the race?
There's joy in every single space.

In the waiting, I find delight,
As clouds drift softly through the night.
They say the early bird sees dawn,
But I've no haste; I'll feast till gone.

A slow blink here, a gentle sigh,
I take my time—oh me, oh my!
The world's a blast while I just chill,
In my tree, I've time to kill.

So let them hurry, let them race,
I'll savor every single place.
With every moment, I'm aware,
Life's best treasures are laid bare.

Serene Spaces of Subdued Fragrance

In branches high, I hang around,
With leafy dreams, where peace is found.
The world rushes by, like a fleeting breeze,
But I take my time, oh, such is my ease.

A gentle yawn, the sun's bright rays,
I could stay here for days and days.
Each fruit a treasure, so ripe and sweet,
I savor slowly, a grand retreat.

Clouds drift lazily, they're on my side,
While busy bees rush, I just abide.
A sip of dew, a midday snack,
In my slow dance, there's no need to track.

The scents of flowers swirl and play,
In my stillness, I find my way.
A pause for thought, a mindful glance,
In this serene space, I take my chance.

The Languid Route to Knowing

A slow ascent, a leisurely climb,
Each branch a thought, taking my time.
With every leaf, a tale unfolds,
Of sunlit days and nights so bold.

The path meanders, a winding song,
I chuckle softly, it won't be long.
The wisdom shared via a gentle sway,
In the subtle breeze, I'm on my way.

While others hurry, I relish the view,
Each moment blissful, each second new.
The art of slowness is where I thrive,
In the dance of stillness, I feel alive.

And when the stars begin to glow,
I'll ponder much; I'll take it slow.
For in this life, a truth I find,
Patience and joy are sweetly entwined.

Meditative Musings from Green Realms

A canvas of green, my home so bright,
Each leaf a whisper, soft and light.
In the heart of trees, I find my muse,
In tranquil thoughts, I cannot lose.

Time stretches forth like shadows at dusk,
In nature's arms, I start to trust.
With every munch, a silent prayer,
In the magic of now, I drift through air.

The rustle of leaves, a soothing sound,
Amongst these giants, peace I've found.
As ants march on, with purpose and speed,
I smile at their rush, but I'll take heed.

The world beneath is full of haste,
While I float softly, a gentle taste.
My thoughts are clouds, they drift and roam,
In these green realms, I feel at home.

The Gentle Pull of Gravity

I hang like a dreamer, safe and sound,
With every sway, the earth's my ground.
Life's little joys, a snack or two,
Gravity's pull, it guides me through.

The world below spins fast and loud,
While I embrace my lazy shroud.
In this slow motion, I find the fun,
Each lazy stretch is a job well done.

The branches cradle, a soft embrace,
While time moves slow, I find my place.
A fluttering leaf drifts down with grace,
In my stillness, I've found my space.

So here I'll linger, beneath the sky,
With clouds for company, stars nearby.
In this gentle pull, I feel quite free,
The art of chilling, just being me.

Embracing the Unhurried

In a world that spins so fast,
I take my time, a contrast.
With every leaf, I find my pace,
In this cozy, leafy space.

I munch on snacks, I take a nap,
Life's a dreamy, gentle trap.
The hurry seems to pass me by,
As clouds drift slowly in the sky.

Why rush when there's a branch to hug?
I swing along just like a slug.
With every yawn, I make my stand,
Zen-like moves in my leafy land.

So join me as we gently glide,
Through lazy days, no need to hide.
Let's charm the hours, it's plain to see,
Unhurried bliss is the key for me.

Reflective Branches

Up high among the leafy trails,
I ponder slow, while sunlight pales.
These branches hold my every thought,
In their embrace, I'm always caught.

The world below rushes like bees,
While I sway softly in the breeze.
Each moment stretches, each sigh expands,
Wisdom whispers through these strands.

What's the hurry, I ask the breeze?
Let's take our time, let time freeze.
Every tick is just surprise,
And time winks back with sleepy eyes.

So nestle in this leafy nest,
Grab a snack, and take a rest.
In this slow-motion, I foresee,
A treasure trove of destiny.

The Joy of Leisurely Moments

I wake up late, the sun is bright,
Yawn and stretch, it feels so right.
With a cucumber on my head,
I chill and laugh, no need for bed.

I shuffle slow, a masterclass,
With every step, I watch the grass.
A leisurely stroll, no rush to roam,
This tree is more than just a home.

The birds hop by, they sing a tune,
While I hang low, enjoying noon.
A little dance, a twirl, a spin,
In my own world, it's where I win.

So here's to moments, slow and grand,
In this warm, embracing land.
With laughter echoing all around,
In my heart, the joy is found.

A Slow Dance with Time

Time glides in with a twirling grace,
I sway along at my own pace.
With every hour, I take a chance,
In this whimsical, undoing dance.

I tiptoe on the edge of dreams,
Where nothing's ever as it seems.
A gentle sway, a sleepy twirl,
In my slow world, I'm just a girl.

With lazy smiles, we twine and twist,
In a rhythm that can't be missed.
Underneath the stars I'll play,
As time whispers, "Stay, just stay."

This tango of tranquility,
A slow embrace, just you and me.
Let's frolic in the moonlit glow,
And celebrate the ebb and flow.

Swaying Through Swathes of Stillness

In the branches I gently sway,
Time is just a game I play.
Leaves above, I often greet,
Taking naps, can't be beat.

Sun shines down, a gentle hug,
I stretch and yawn, then give a shrug.
Clouds drift by in a lazy dance,
Why rush when there's time to prance?

Worms wiggle by, I wave hello,
They seem so fast; where do they go?
But here I hang, enjoying my view,
Each inch moves like a grand debut.

Soon the day will softly close,
With sleepy sighs, and gentle doze.
In my world, there's no big fuss,
Just hang around and make a plus.

The Unfolding of Subtle Life

My leafy home, a cozy space,
In stillness, I've found my place.
Nature hums a soothing tune,
I dance, but that's just my boon.

Fuzzy toes in the summer sun,
While others rush, I just have fun.
With a blink, the world goes fast,
In my world, we make it last.

Breezes whisper sweet delights,
As I relax and count the heights.
Watch the ants march in a line,
For them, I just sip on pine.

Oh, the joy in simple things,
Like munching leaves or flapping wings.
Every moment, a treasure, oh so grand,
What's your hurry? Let's just stand!

A Tranquil Tapestry of Existence

Up high, I weave my cozy web,
Stitched with dreams, a vibrant ebb.
The world below is bustling by,
But here, I'm free to laugh and sigh.

The sun yawns, kissing trees alight,
Colorful hues make my day bright.
With each blink, I savor the scene,
Why rush when I can just be keen?

Raindrops tap like a gentle tune,
I hum along, beneath the moon.
Nature's brush paints all around,
In my slow dance, joy is profound.

Each hanging moment, a treasure trove,
In this slow dance, I find my grove.
Let others dash, I'll sip my tea,
And perfect this sweet harmony.

Delight in the Drowsy

Waking up, what a stretch, oh dear!
A morning nap? Now that's sincere.
With a blissful grin, I sway around,
In my drowsy world, joy is found.

Sunscreen made of leaves and sap,
In this sleepy zone, there's no mishap.
Rivers flow, while I just chill,
The art of doing nothing is quite the thrill.

Gazing up at the clouds above,
Matching shapes, that's what I love.
A turtle trots, I offer a wave,
But in my heart, it's rest I crave.

Evening falls with a sleepy sigh,
Stars twinkle as I nibble a spry.
Delight in drowsy, I softly beam,
In the realm of peace, I softly dream.

The Subtlety of Still Moments

Time drips slow like honey,
The world zips, but I just chill.
A nap is my favorite journey,
Dreaming of the next big meal.

Branches sway, the sun peeks through,
I hang like a question mark.
While others rush, I take my cue,
To savor every tiny spark.

Blossoming in the Quiet

Petals fall in soft ballet,
Colors dance, but I stay still.
In this moment, I play,
Absorbing good vibes at my will.

From my perch, I watch the show,
Life's a stage, and I'm backstage.
No reason to rush, just flow,
As the world turns another page.

Suspended in Nature's Tempo

I'm a glider through green leaves,
Embracing time like a warm hug.
While others hustle, fret, and weave,
I sip the breeze, feeling snug.

Nature's clock ticks at my pace,
No deadlines, just sweet refrain.
In this leisurely, cozy space,
Every moment feels like gain.

Poised for Reflection

Gazing down from lofty heights,
Thoughts drift like clouds in the sky.
In the stillness, I find delights,
As I just hang and sigh.

Like a pause in a lively song,
I relish silence in between.
In nature's arms, where I belong,
Finding joy in moments unseen.

A Journey Through Verdant Minutes

In the canopy, I sway and grin,
Each slow-motion moment, a gentle win.
Branches cradle dreams with leafy care,
While the world rushes by, I lounge with flair.

The clock ticks softly, a whispering friend,
Counting seconds that barely extend.
I ponder the art of taking it slow,
As butterflies drift, and breezes flow.

With every blink, I stretch and sigh,
Watching clouds parade in the vast blue sky.
Life's a feast when you take your time,
A symphony played, in a blissful rhyme.

So here I hang, with no need to chase,
In a world where speed finds no embrace.
Joy grows in pauses, not in the dash,
As I munch on leaves, and let moments splash.

Savoring Every Leaf

With each green morsel, I relish and chew,
In the great expanse, I find my brew.
Leaves like curtains, flutter and sway,
In the grand theater, I enjoy the play.

Every bite speaks tales of trees and sun,
Nature's snacks are delicious fun.
While others gulp down their hurried meals,
I take my time, savor what appeals.

The world may whirl in a frenzied dance,
But I languidly slip into a trance.
Life's complexities become absurd,
When you relish each leaf, undeterred.

So here I munch, while my friends ask why,
I don't race around like a bee on the fly.
In the art of chewing, joy's interleaved,
With thoughts of the next leaf, I'm quite pleased.

The Art of Not Rushing

In a world where haste is all the rage,
I set my pace, turn a new page.
Like a cozy book with a gentle plot,
I take it slow, forget the fraught.

Raindrops fall like slow applause,
As I pause to wonder, without a cause.
Nature speaks in whispers, clear and bright,
While time stretches out, like a lazy kite.

Oh, to be still, like a leaf in the breeze,
I twirl with glee, while others appease.
With a yawn and a stretch, I unwind my thoughts,
Finding joy in the slow, that speed forgot.

So let them rush; let the world spin around,
I'm content in my slowness, blissfully unbound.
For in every slow moment, I discover delight,
A mellow heartbeat beneath the twilight.

Slowly Unraveling Time

In the tapestry of time, I weave my thread,
Each second's a fiber, gentle instead.
With each inch I climb, I twist and curl,
My leisurely stroll is a joyous whirl.

Clouds drift like dreams, past shadows and light,
While I cling to branches, feeling just right.
A sloth's delight in a carefree quest,
Turning every moment into a fest.

Ticking clocks mean nothing in this grand game,
As I lounge and ponder, the world is the same.
Why hurry to finish when the journey is gold?
With each passing breeze, new stories unfold.

So here I hang, the master of chill,
Unraveling time with a laugh, and a thrill.
For in this slow dance, I truly find,
The wonders of moments that may unwind.

Tranquil Teachings on the Wind

In the canopy high, I slowly sway,
Leaves whisper secrets in the light of day.
Why rush and scurry when time's a friend?
I'll take my time, the fun never ends.

With a yawn so wide, the world unfolds,
Stories in branches, adventures untold.
Each moment I savor, each breath I take,
Why leap through life when I can partake?

The clouds drift by, painting skies with glee,
I stretch out my limbs, so blissfully free.
Every slow move, a dance with the breeze,
In my leafy perch, I do as I please.

So heed my wise ways, let laughter arise,
Savor your snacks and relish the skies.
For at my own pace, joy comes right through,
With leisurely thoughts, the world's brand new.

The Slumbering Spirit of the Forest

Nestled in branches, my thoughts float like air,
While creatures around me rush here and there.
With a sleepy smile, I look down below,
Why hurry through life when it moves so slow?

A snail passes by, I nod with a grin,
In the game's own time, I'm always the win.
The more that I linger, the fun that I find,
Life's sweetest moments come gently aligned.

In dappled sunlight, the world's soft embrace,
My eyelids grow heavy; it's time for a race.
A race to the dreams where we float on the leaves,
Where laughter and joy are the ultimate keys.

So here I shall stay, in my wonky retreat,
Enjoying the calm, my own special beat.
Join in this fun, let your spirit unwind,
For deep in the woods, it's peace you will find.

Meandering Through Meadows of Mindfulness

Wandering slowly through fields of delight,
Each blade of grass welcomes me, oh what a sight!
With every small lap, I embrace the gist,
Of being so present, not letting it twist.

The daisies dance, as I wander about,
"Hey, slow down!" the sun seems to shout.
But I laugh in return, no reason for haste,
In this playful stroll, there's no time to waste.

Butterflies flutter, they giggle and glide,
While I'm lost in the rhythm, the gentle tide.
Moments stretch wide, like my afternoon snack,
With nature around, there's nothing I lack.

So follow my lead, let tranquility reign,
While laughter drifts soft as a patter of rain.
In each happy moment, we'll take our sweet time,
And dance through the meadows, in perfect rhyme.

Epiphanies at Dusk

As twilight descends, so too do my thoughts,
Like fireflies flickering in their own spots.
Each shimmer a lesson from nature, it seems,
Isn't slow soaking up the best of our dreams?

I ponder the stars while I dangle serene,
Life's simple rules wrapped in twilight's sheen.
Why sprint through the chapters when each page can wait?
Moments are treasures; let's not tempt fate.

The moon's silver glow stretches wide in the sky,
While crickets compose their soft lullaby.
A giggle escapes from my leafy retreat,
For slow is the dance, and it's oh so sweet.

So cherish the dusk, oh delightful affair,
With each cozy sigh, sprinkle love in the air.
For the fun lies not just in what we pursue,
But in the small joys—forever in view.

The World Through Drowsy Eyes

In the trees I slowly sway,
Every branch my cozy bay.
Sunlight filters, soft and low,
What's the rush? I'll take it slow.

Birds are singing, I'll yawn wide,
While the world zips by outside.
Why not hang here, take a snooze?
There's no race, just time to choose.

I'll watch the leaves that gently fall,
Every second a lazy call.
With each blink, the hours fade,
In this tranquil, leafy shade.

So let them hurry, let them race,
In my tree, I've found my space.
Life's a slow, delightful ride,
In my arms, all peace resides.

Time in the Gentle Grip of Green

Underneath the boughs I fold,
In a world that's soft and old.
Tangled vines and murky streams,
Time drips down like sweetened dreams.

One twig snaps, a bug goes by,
I half-watch it, then say bye.
Mossy whispers tickle my ear,
Night's cool breath is creeping near.

Each hour takes a lazy stroll,
As I munch on leaves, my goal.
What's it like to run around?
I'm the king of this fine ground.

So let the sun dip low and bounce,
I'll hang here, giving nature a pounce.
With a flick of my sleepy paw,
I embrace this world, filled with awe.

A Symphony of Soporific Serenity

The symphony of sleepy tones,
Is played by leaves and whispered groans.
Each breeze a lullaby so sweet,
In my home, I find my beat.

Beneath the vast and azure dome,
All my thoughts drift slowly home.
The rustle of the world outside,
Is but a faint and sleepy tide.

Nutty dreams come slip and slide,
As I sway from side to side.
With every twinkle in the sky,
I play my part and let time fly.

Harmony in drowsy ways,
Each moment's worth, a gentle praise.
I find my joy in quiet sights,
In slothful dreams, my heart ignites.

Paws on the Path of Purpose

With each paw placed oh so slow,
I navigate this world's grand show.
Not a hurry, but a sway,
Every step, a chance to play.

I see them rushing, what a sight!
Glimpses of a frantic flight.
Yet here I am, enjoying still,
Every moment, what a thrill!

As I munch on leaves divine,
Time is simply a friend of mine.
Each little pause, a step so grand,
In my slow and gentle land.

Purpose isn't always fast,
It's those moments, meant to last.
I'm the guardian of my tree,
In my heart, I'm always free.

Revelations from the Canopy

Up high in the trees, I ponder slow,
Time ticks by like a gentle flow.
Branches sway, my thoughts unwind,
In a world that rushes, I'm blissfully blind.

With each lazy stretch, I find my glee,
Why hurry when snacks dangle free?
The sun's warm hug, a soft embrace,
A perfect moment, my favorite place.

Leaves whisper secrets, soft and low,
As I droop my limbs, with nowhere to go.
Racing? Not me; I'll pass on that,
This golden hour beats a sprinting cat.

And should I yawn under the sky's dome,
Guess what? I've already made it home!
To savor each second, this is my creed,
In the tree tops, I take the lead.

The Zen of Hanging Around

Chillin' with the breeze, life's such a breeze,
No deadlines here, just soft, swaying leaves.
With a slight twist, I stretch and yawn,
With each lazy blink, a new day is born.

Why scurry and fuss? Where's the thrill?
I sip on the sun and take in the chill.
In this cozy nook, worries subside,
The art of just hanging, my ultimate pride.

A slow-motion day, oh what a delight,
Dreaming of snacks 'neath the pale moonlight.
Between munches and naps, I find my groove,
With every moment, I slowly move.

As shadows stretch long, I sway in the breeze,
Wishing all humans could learn this with ease.
Every second counts, but in my domain,
The slow road is best—why race in vain?

Shadows of a Sated Soul

In the quiet dusk, I find my tune,
Underneath a lazy, brightening moon.
Belly full of leaves, a happy sigh,
Today's worries just drift on by.

I lounge in my tree, sprawled out wide,
The world below, it's a joyous ride.
Took my time to feast, no need for haste,
With each slow bite, I savor the taste.

Friends zip by, oh, what a show!
But sloths know the secret: take it slow.
Moments are treasures, tucked in a fold,
Wrapped in the warmth of stories retold.

When dusk settles in, it brings peace anew,
In my leafy home, dreams all come true.
So here I shall stay, in blissful control,
Basking in shadows, a sated soul.

Embracing the Art of Idleness

Oh what joy in the art of delay,
While friends dash around, I'll choose to stay.
With limbs stretched long, in cozy embrace,
I paint my world at my own gentle pace.

The dance of the leaves makes me feel whole,
In the peace of the treetops, I've found my role.
Who needs a rush? What's the big race?
I'm an expert in chilling, my favorite space.

Sipping sunlight, a natural brew,
Letting each second casually ensue.
In this hammock of time, I finally see,
The secret of joy lies in being free.

So here's to the dreamers who linger long,
To each idle moment, you'll find where you belong.
In a world that spins, let the sloths lead,
For happiness blooms in a slow-paced seed.

A Patience Built in Paws

In the tree's slow embrace, I lounge,
The world rushes by, but I frown,
'Why the hurry?' I often ponder,
While I nap, they grow old, I wander.

With each tiny leaf, a treasure found,
A snack that makes my heart resound,
My tempo's set to a glorious crawl,
In my fuzzy realm, I reign overall.

The sun climbs high, then starts to sink,
I stretch my limbs, stop to think,
Each day's adventure takes its cue,
From the squirrels who zoom, how about you?

I'll climb, I'll munch, then snooze some more,
As time drifts by, I explore,
With laughter echoing through the trees,
In this slow dance, I'm wholly at ease.

Discovering Depths of Drowsiness

Awake or asleep, I can't really say,
As dreams and reality play in the fray,
With half-lidded eyes, I sway in a daze,
Tangled in thoughts, like a sloth in a gaze.

Who needs a rush when you can recline?
A world full of wonders I'll simply divine,
Tick tock is a joke, just take it real slow,
For happiness lies in the chill of the flow.

Through the fluffy clouds, I drift and I dream,
In snoozy daytimes, life's sweeter than cream,
Each yawn like a symphony, soft in its thread,
I stretch, then I munch, and back to my bed.

So come join the dance, it's never too late,
In the cozy embrace where we contemplate,
For in this warm luster, all worries subside,
As drowsiness reigns, we let joy be our guide.

Contemplative Views from Above

Perched high on my branch, the world is a show,
With birds singing tunes, and breezes that blow,
I notice the chaos that passes me by,
And chuckle at folks rushing; oh my, oh my!

Down below, they bustle, a colorful race,
While I take my time, a slow-motion grace,
Have they never seen how the leaves spin and sway?
It's a dance of serenity, a blissful ballet.

With a grin on my face, I enjoy my view,
Nature's comedy hour plays just for a few,
As I munch on the greens, my heart feels so light,
What's better than lounging from morning till night?

So why not pause, and breathe in the trees?
Join me in laughter, enjoy the sweet breeze,
For while the world rushes with every sweet song,
There's joy in the stillness; let's all get along.

Darting Leaves, Drifting Thoughts

Amidst fluttering leaves, I pause for a snack,
With every small bite, I lose track of the pack,
The winds dance around, in a fluttering race,
While I settle down in my cozy embrace.

Squirrels will mock as they zoom here and there,
But I've got the secret—they're missing the flair,
For in each drowsy moment, I find joy anew,
In the art of just being, I'm right on cue.

Leaves swirl through the air like a sweet serenade,
While I watch from my perch, a sloth masquerade,
With dreams of slow drifting and time that's our friend,
It's a party of stillness, where the giggles don't end.

So let them all dash, and let them all race,
I'll savor the moments, no need to keep pace,
For darting leaves, oh what a show,
While drifting through thoughts is where happiness grows.

Wisdom in Every Yawn

Each stretch reveals a secret thought,
The world can wait, it's not distraught.
With every yawn, a gentle sigh,
Slow down, my friend, just let it lie.

In a race? Not my kind of game,
I'll savor sleep, it's not the same.
The wisdom found in snoozing deep,
Is worth much more than losing sleep.

Hanging Out in the Sunlight

With limbs like branches, I find my spot,
A sunny perch, oh, how time's forgot!
The ants march past, all quick and spry,
But here in warmth, I'll just comply.

A leisurely gaze at clouds so high,
A gentle breeze sings me a lullaby.
Why rush around when sunbeams gleam?
I'd rather nap than chase a dream.

The Beauty of Being Unfazed

Through stormy skies or sunny haze,
I move at my own pace, always stays.
With a twitch of my ear, life goes on,
While others fret from dusk till dawn.

The world may spin in dizzying speed,
But I embrace each lazy deed.
A slip, a slide, what's the big fuss?
It's just a stumble; no need to rush.

Slumbering in the Shade

The leaves above are swaying slow,
While I'm beneath, in blanket flow.
A soft caress from nature's hand,
In quietude, I make my stand.

With drowsy dreams and cozy nooks,
I ponder life, read nature's books.
Here in the shade, the world feels right,
As snores echo softly, goodnight, goodnight!

Delicate Rhythms of a Relaxed Heart

In the canopy, I sway with ease,
Chasing dreams with a gentle breeze.
Time's a friend who loves to tease,
Each moment savored like fine cheese.

Cuddled close in my leafy bed,
Resting my thoughts, no need for dread.
Sunshine's warmth, the pillow spread,
I sing sweet songs while others tread.

Branches dance, my mind takes flight,
Stars above keep me in sight.
Naps by day and joy each night,
My heartbeats slow, my soul feels light.

A life that teeters on delight,
In every leaf, a laugh takes flight.
With every yawn, the world feels bright,
Savoring moments, oh what a sight!

The Philosophy of Slow

Why rush when I can play it cool?
The world's a grand and goofy school.
Each slow step feels like a jewel,
I'm the master of my own rule.

With toothy grins, I take my time,
Climbing high seems like a crime.
A sunny spot is my prime,
Joy in stillness, so sublime!

As others race to reach the top,
I'm rolling gently; I won't stop.
With silly thoughts, I laugh and plop,
To see the wonders, oh what a hop!

I ponder deep in leafy shrouds,
Beneath the branches, away from crowds.
My slow dance gathers fluffy clouds,
In the stillness, laughter loud!

Unhurried Hues of Harmony

The colors swirl, a vibrant show,
In slow-mo wonders, watch them glow.
I chart my path as I take it slow,
In every shade, there's time to grow.

With every munch, I find my beat,
Healthy snacks, oh such a treat.
Nature's rhythm, oh so sweet,
I sway and groove to the leafy heat.

Even the clouds drift on by,
My heart's at peace, don't ask me why.
I wave to the birds as they fly high,
And greet each moment with a sigh.

So here I twirl in nature's art,
Life's a picnic, I take my part.
With every nap, I feel the start,
Of joyful days that fill my heart!

Embracing Every Leafy Moment

I hang around, not much to do,
Beneath the trees, the sky so blue.
With leafy pals, I'll bid adieu,
To racing thoughts that fly right through.

Each gust of wind, a friendly tease,
I just chill out, enjoy the breeze.
Life's a puzzle, take it with ease,
I'm on a quest for nachos and cheese!

With each new branch, I find delight,
Swinging softly from day to night.
Savoring flavors, oh what a sight,
In every moment, pure joy takes flight.

So here's my motto, soft and clear,
Slow down, my friend, just persevere.
Seek the fun, the snacks, the cheer,
And in that dance, you'll find good beer!

Journey of the Joyful Snoozer

In the branches high, I sway with ease,
A nap so sweet, it's a gentle breeze.
Time rolls by, with no rush in sight,
A slothful dance under warm sunlight.

With every yawn, my worries fade,
Dreams of munching on leaves relayed.
Why rush ahead when I can chill?
A slow-motion joy, that's my thrill!

My friends zoom past, in a wild flurry,
But I just smile, no need to hurry.
For in my world, each moment's gold,
A cozy life, as the stories unfold.

So here I hang, with a silly grin,
In my slow-paced wonder, I always win.
Each sleepy day is a treasure trove,
A joyful journey, where I freely rove.

Pondering Life from the Branches

Hanging here, I think of the world,
As leaves all around me slowly twirled.
What's the rush, I ponder with glee,
While ants march by, in a hurry to flee.

Each slow blink unveils a new thought,
Why worry about what can't be caught?
In this slow lane, time bends and flows,
A melody soft, as the cool wind blows.

The branches sway to a lullaby,
While clouds drift lazy through the sky.
I contemplate life from my leafy nook,
With no agenda, just my cozy book.

A wise sloth knows that here in the trees,
The answers come with a gentle breeze.
So let the world rush on by, I say,
I'll stick to my ponder, and nap the day away.

The Comfort of Delayed Dreams

I move so slow, like a leaf in flight,
With dreams that twinkle, oh so bright.
Why chase the dawn, when dusk feels right?
In my slow rhythm, I find delight.

Snuggled up tight in my leafy bed,
I savor each thought that dances in my head.
Tomorrow's a mystery, but that's okay,
Today's all I need to enjoy my stay.

Oh, the thrill of indulging in z's,
While the world rushes on, a flurry of bees.
Delayed desires, I embrace with glee,
For patient hearts thrive; it's plain to see.

So here I lounge, in my slow-motion scheme,
Relishing moments and savoring dreams.
With every yawn, a treasure's found,
In the thrill of delay, true joy abounds.

Unfurling Thoughts in the Twilight

As the sun dips low, I stretch my limbs,
Thoughts unfurl like rhythmic hymns.
Twilight whispers of secrets old,
In this magical hour, I let unfold.

Each lazy moment glides on by,
With shimmering stars sparkling high.
In the twilight glow, I ponder deep,
Where dreams are planted and memories keep.

What's faster than time, I muse aloud,
While I hang out amongst the cloud.
Laugh lines deepen with every tease,
In this peaceful pace, where I seize.

As the night wraps around with a smile,
I nestle in thoughts for a little while.
With giggles and sighs, my worries melt,
In twilight's embrace, so warmly felt.

The Art of Suspended Moments

Hanging high, I take my time,
The world rushes by, a silly rhyme.
Too slow to care, in slow-motion bliss,
Every leaf is a treasure, I surely can't miss.

My days are painted in shades of green,
A clock that ticks only when unseen.
While others scurry, I simply chew,
To ponder the mysteries, all brand new.

With a yawn so grand, I stretch my toes,
Why go fast when the sunshine glows?
Like a painter to canvas, I linger and pause,
In the art of doing nothing, I find my cause.

So when life's a race, just take it slow,
Join me in the branches, let worries go.
For in each suspended moment, a gift is found,
A delight in the quiet, no pressure around.

Leisurely Lessons from a Languid Luminary

In tree-top schools, I teach my ways,
Of napping long through sunny days.
The lesson's simple, take a rest,
It's the art of sloth, we do it best.

With a smile so wide, I eat my leaves,
While others rush, my chill achieves.
The secret's out: relax, don't stress,
In the grand race, I'm truly blessed.

Every hour's a chance to snooze,
In cuddly silence, who could refuse?
When the wind whispers through my fur,
I giggle softly, oh how I purr.

So come with me to a slower pace,
Find joy in moments — that's the case.
With laughter echoing through the trees,
Life's a feast of giggles, if you please!

In the Embrace of Stillness

In dappled sunlight, I find my grace,
The art of stillness, my happy space.
With every branch, I find my seat,
In a world of chaos, it feels so sweet.

Leaves flutter gently, time stands still,
Each droplet of dew, a moment to fill.
Why rush and race through the hustle and flow?
I'd rather enjoy this sweet, mellow show.

So raise your arms, let out a sigh,
Join me as we simply lie.
With a lazy stretch, oh what a thrill,
In the embrace of stillness, let's just chill.

With clouds floating by, we watch the game,
As the world speeds up, we stay the same.
In laughter, we bask under the sky,
For nothing beats sloth, oh my, oh my!

Woolly Wisdom of the Tree-Dweller

High in the trees, my wisdom blooms,
In fluffy furs, I conquer glooms.
Slowly I ponder, with a twinkle of mirth,
Lessons of sloth, straight from the earth.

What's life without laughter, a hug, a thrill?
Why rush to 'do' when you can just 'chill'?
With a tilt of my head, wisdom flows,
In the dance of slowness, anything goes.

I giggle at haste, it all seems so mad,
In my quiet world, I never feel bad.
If life feels a race, take it down a notch,
In every still moment, find your sweet spot.

For I am the keeper of lightly-spun dreams,
In the tapestry of trees, I weave with beams.
With a heart full of chuckles and soul made from fun,
What joy it is, just to dangle and run!

Deliberate Steps to Destiny

In a world that rushes fast,
I take each step, never last.
With a yawn and a gentle sway,
I ponder life in my own way.

While others sprint and chase the sun,
I lounge around, I'm having fun.
Every leaf, a tasty cone,
I savor all, I stroll alone.

Why stress my thoughts with burdens wide?
I'm happiest with time as my guide.
With my slow dance, I must confess,
A happy heart knows no distress.

So join me in this lazy quest,
Where speed is fate, but I digress.
In each deliberate step I take,
I weave a path that none can break.

Arrayed in Green, Mellow and Free

Draped in leaves of emerald hue,
In sweet stillness, I find my cue.
Life is quaint, a verdant brew,
I stretch my limbs, yet never do.

A flick of tongue, a snack divine,
In this canopy, I simply dine.
While others bustle fast and fume,
I bloom like flowers in soft plume.

My friends may bound, they leap and dart,
But I've got nature's soothing art.
With laughter soft like rustling trees,
I linger in the gentle breeze.

Arrayed in green, I take my seat,
With leaves around, my heart skips a beat.
Here, every moment seems to sway,
Mellow and free, I greet the day.

Thoughts Cocooned in Stillness

Nestled high on branches thick,
I ponder truths, both deep and quick.
In this cocoon of leafy dreams,
I find delight in silent schemes.

While others race, consumed by haste,
I take it slow, I savor taste.
With each slow blink, a thought unfurls,
In whispered winds, my mind twirls.

Ideas creeping like the vines,
They twist and turn in playful lines.
In stillness found, I craft my art,
A masterpiece from beating heart.

So stop and pause, just take a glance,
In tranquil thoughts, there's room to dance.
Cocooned and calm, I greet the swell,
Of life's soft secrets, under spell.

Melodies of the Unhurried Soul

In the quiet, my spirit sings,
A melody of simple things.
With every hum, a gentle breeze,
I sway along with rustling leaves.

Each note a drop of morning dew,
I let it linger, soft and true.
While chaos rages all around,
I'm the calm in sound profound.

My rhythm flows with nature's beat,
Not hurried, but oh so sweet.
I dance in sync with sunlit beams,
Creating symphonies of dreams.

So join me in this lazy stroll,
Where time's a friend, and hearts are whole.
In melodies of soft embrace,
The unhurried find their sacred space.

Daydreams at a Snail's Pace

In a tree so high, I slowly sway,
Dreaming of adventures, come what may.
With every blink, the world does pause,
A snack of leaves, my only cause.

Time trickles down like honey thick,
Why run when you can do the trick?
The clouds float by, a cotton candy treat,
Life's a feast, oh, isn't that sweet?

I ponder stars while sunbeams fade,
Chasing shadows, a daring trade.
Slow is the route, no need for haste,
In this grand ballet, it's all a taste.

So if you rush, just take a cue,
From this sloth up in the blue.
With giggles echoing through the trees,
I'll nap and snack, it's how I seize!

The Quietude of Life's Climb

Climbing high, oh what a sight,
The world below, a disco light.
I hang out here, no stress to find,
Enjoying peace that's unconfined.

Each branch a step, so slow and sweet,
I stop to greet the morning greet.
No rush for me, just one more leaf,
In this quietude, there's no grief.

Gentle whispers in the tree,
A world where time just lets me be.
With each soft breeze, I stand so still,
This is my realm, my heart's own thrill.

So when you stumble on rocky trails,
Remember this sloth who lifts the veils.
For quiet climbs bring joy's embrace,
In every moment, find your place.

Gentle Paths of Existence

Life's a path with twists and turns,
As I slide, my spirit yearns.
With every munch and every snooze,
In this slow dance, I cannot lose.

Strolling gently beneath the sun,
My day's agenda? Just some fun!
A munch of leaves, a friendly leaf,
In this lazy state, there's no grief.

The winds may blow, but I won't budge,
With nature's rhythm, I'll always judge.
Who needs the rush or frantic chase?
My heart beats softly, a gentle pace.

So if you wonder about the haste,
Join in my groove, just take a taste.
For gentle paths have much to share,
Ride the slow wave and breathe the air.

Navigating Life's Low Branches

I tiptoe through the leafy shade,
Low branches bend, a leafy braid.
With careful moves, I seek my route,
In every branch, a sweet pursuit.

Wobbling slightly, I jump and sway,
Who said that slow is dull, I say?
Falling leaves dance all around,
A symphony without a sound.

Each branch a lesson, soft and slow,
In this game of life, I steal the show.
Navigating all with style and grace,
With gentle smiles, I find my place.

So if you're feeling like you're stuck,
Channel my groove, it's not bad luck.
For low branches lead us to the sky,
In this journey, we all can fly!

Time's Soft Mirage

In the tree, I make my stand,
Counting seconds, oh so grand.
The world rushes, what a scene,
But I just chill, if you know what I mean.

With every yawn, I take it slow,
Watching clouds like they're in a show.
Time's a trickster, soft and sly,
While I munch leaves and sigh, oh my!

The sun drifts by, a slow parade,
I'm here basking, unafraid.
Why hurry when you can just float?
A cozy branch is my happy boat!

As I doze and take my time,
The frantic chase feels like a crime.
So here's my tip, my dear fast friends:
Just pause a bit, and time transcends.

Hanging Out with Harmony

Swinging softly, what a thrill,
Nature's rhythm fits the bill.
I groove to sounds of wind and light,
Finding joy in every bite.

With lazy grins and gentle hugs,
I make my home with all the bugs.
The world can spin, whizz, and zoom,
But here, I'm safe—no hint of gloom.

Life's a jam, and I'm the tune,
In this green room, I'll sway and swoon.
So grab a branch, let the fun unfold,
With slothlike grace, watch stories told.

Every moment's bold, yet sweet,
In this hanging place, I'm hard to beat.
Slowly smiling through the day,
Let's laugh together — come what may!

Grace in Glacial Motion

Step by step, I take my pace,
Painting time with my own grace.
While others rush with wild ambition,
I find bliss in a gentle mission.

Let the world whirl and fizz about,
I prefer stillness—no doubt!
Each leaf I munch, a grand delight,
Taking my time feels just right.

With every stretch, I strike a pose,
Elegance grows as the laughter flows.
Wobbling slowly, I'll claim my fame,
In this slow dance, I'm not to blame!

So here I sway, oh so divine,
Living my truth, and sipping fine.
Embrace the slow, let worries pass,
In this gentle world, we'll have a blast!

Swaying in the Breeze of Being

Sway with me in leafy dreams,
Where sunlight spills and soft wind streams.
I'll take my time, yes I confess,
This slow existence is my success.

A twist, a turn, a playful stretch,
In this cozy spot, there's no sketch.
Beneath the shade, I look and see,
Every moment is wild and free.

Join the dance, don't be in haste,
Life's a picnic, let's not waste.
With a gentle bounce, we'll find our glee,
Embracing the pause, just you and me.

So let's sway in this tender breeze,
Laughing joy through the swaying trees.
In the dance of calm, we'll forever glide,
With slothful joy, let the world take its ride!

www.ingramcontent.com/pod-product-compliance
Lightning Source LLC
Chambersburg PA
CBHW051659160426
43209CB00004B/960